Business Growth Strategies

The Path TO Building Your Tribe

For Newbie Entrepreneurs

By: Kameron J. Alexander

Alexander Network Digital

All Rights Reserved!

ALL RIGHTS RESERVED. No part of this report may be modified or altered in any form whatsoever, electronic, or mechanical, including photocopying, recording, or by any informational storage or retrieval system without express written, dated and signed permission from the author.

AFFILIATE DISCLAIMER. The short, direct, non-legal version is this: Some of the links in this report may be affiliate links which means that I earn money if you choose to buy from that vendor at some point in the near future. I do not choose which products and services to promote based upon which pay me the most, I choose based upon my decision of which I would recommend to a dear friend. You will never pay more for an item by clicking through my affiliate link, and, in fact, may pay less since I negotiate special offers for my readers that are not available elsewhere.

DISCLAIMER AND/OR LEGAL NOTICES: The information presented herein represents the view of the author as of the date of publication. Because of the rate with which conditions change, the author reserves the right to alter and update his opinion based on the new conditions. The report is for informational purposes only. While every attempt has been made to verify the information provided in this report, neither the author nor his affiliates/partners assume any responsibility for errors, inaccuracies, or omissions. Any slights of people or organizations are unintentional. If advice concerning legal or related matters is needed, the services of a fully qualified professional should be sought. This report is not intended for use as a source of legal or accounting advice. You should be aware of any laws which govern business transactions or other business practices in your country and state. Any reference to any person or business whether living or dead is purely coincidental.

Copyright © Alexander Network Digital
www.thealexandernetworkdigital.com
ISBN (Paperback) 978-1-7374637-6-4
Book Cover by: Thornton Online Marketing LLC

Acknowledgments

First, I want to thank my lord and savior who is the head of my life. Giving me the strength to step out on faith and go for my dream. Without him, none of this would be possible I thank him in advance for what he has done and what he is going to do in not only me and my family's life but, you and your family's life as well.

I want to say, I am very happy that you took this step and invested in yourself. That lets me know that you are serious about taking your brand or business to the next level whatever that may be for you. And I believe in you and the vision that will come from reading these Business Growth Strategies. There are a few people I would like to thank on this journey of building my business and brand.

I would like to thank my beautiful wife for sticking with me on this journey. Lord knows it's not an easy task of consistency and dedication. With all the late nights and early mornings, you have always been there with love and support. I want to let you know that I love you and appreciate you being there with your love and support. You always are there to let me know that you believe in me and that I can do anything when I put God first. Thank you for being my backbone for me and the kids. I love and appreciate your love and support.

  To my kids just want to say thank you for helping me become a better son, father, and husband. Without you guys, I would not be who I am today for sure. I just want to say I can't wait to see what the future holds for you and the sky is no limit. I love you and appreciate you for helping me become the men I am today.

  I want to show my appreciation to my Mom (Audra Webb) and Pops (Rev. Clifford Webb). Thank you for being there and giving me a word of encouragement. Mom, thank you for supporting me in all of my learning processes. Pops thanks for supporting me as well you have always been there to lift me when I was feeling down or not encouraged. Just want to say I appreciate your encouraging words of wisdom and love you both.

Finally, my mentors, I want to thank all my mentors for helping me stretch. Becoming comfortable with being uncomfortable and stretching into my full potential. To all my current and future mentors, I appreciate everything you have done to help me grow and stretch into someone that can help others. Stretch and grow into a powerful force. Seeing that it is ok to trust the process and not rush the process.

Contents

Business Growth Strategies 1
Section 1: Building Your Brand 7
    What Is a Brand? 8
    Why You Should Build a Brand? 11
    The power Of a Brand 13
    The 6 Steps to Build a Brand 14
Section 2: Building an effective business plan 27
    Why Do You Need a Business Plan? 28
    Before We Get Started 31
    9 Elements of a Business Plan 34
        Build Your Dream Business Plan 55
Section 3: Building Your Tribe 58
    The Age of The Influencers 59
    What Is an Influencer? 60
        Platforms For Influencers 62
        Benefits of Being an Influencer 64
    9 Strategies to Building a Tribe 66
The Conclusion 91
Additional Resources 95

Section 1: Building Your Brand

What Is a Brand?

A brand is much more than just a flashy logo or color scheme. A brand goes way past having a good-looking business card. A brand is not only about having a website with your name on it, even though that is an important part of it. A brand is way bigger than keeping things to yourself. It's more so about who you are and what you do. Your brand is how you present yourself, both online and offline, to your tribe and community.

Your brand is what's being shown first in front and center. It's presenting to the world, the core of who you or your business is as a person or entity. It's like the secret sauce that makes your business different from everyone else.

Your brand includes your:

- Values
- Unique Skills
- Experiences
- Stories
- Personality

- Image

All these must be presented as your authentic self. Your brand centers around you as a person or business. It's about what you bring to the table, the value that you offer. The specific ways you solve people's deepest pain points and biggest frustrations. You may be thinking that's only for big companies, which is not true anymore. We have the internet and social media. With the power of those, anyone can build their brand. We can add value to their tribe at any time. We can communicate our message loud and clear. We can constantly put ourselves in front of our tribe. We now have the tools to build powerful brands.

Whether you know it or not, everyone has a brand whether they like it or not. Like me for example I was known as the quiet cool kid in high school. Now, the question becomes are you actively in control of your brand, or is it in control of you? Everything you do ties back to you and your brand. It all shapes what people think of you and the image you put out.

How do you build a brand? How do you get in control of the process? How do you make sure your brand is helping build your business?

Why You Should Build a Brand?

You're probably thinking by now why do I need to build a brand? I'm not one of those big companies, I'm not a celebrity, why do I need to build a brand. The reality is every business whether you're an owner, freelancer, consultant, entrepreneur, etc., should be building its brand. If you are building a business of any sort, it's important to build your brand around it. You don't have to be a big company or a celebrity for you to benefit from building a brand.

Let's see what some of the benefits are when building a brand:

- Allows you to stand out from the competition
    - Experiences, strengths, beliefs, perspectives, skills, and insights highlighting your uniqueness
- Allows you to charge a premium price
    - Bringing your unique value allows you to charge premium prices for your services
- Highlights what you're good at

- The more valuable the content shared the more you show that you're an expert who can be trusted. Proving that you are the go-to person in your industry.
- Allows you to attract your ideal tribe
  - attracting you to people who need your help the most
- Connects you with more individuals
  - Truth is that people connect more with the person than the actual company

The power Of a Brand

Are you starting to see the power of your brand? Your brand is what enables you to recognize yourself from the competition. It allows you to charge those premium prices for your services. The more focused you are on your brand, the more knowledgeable you become, and the more you become a known expert in your field. The more you're known as an expert, the more opportunities come your way.

The more you build your brand, the more you connect with others, which in turn builds your business even more. I think it's safe to say that there are a few things more powerful than your brand. The more you focus on building it the greater your results will be. Now, are you ready to start building your brand?

The 6 Steps to Build a Brand

Now that you know why you should be building a brand. Let's break down some different steps and strategies you can use to build your powerful brand.

Step #1 Determine Who You Are

The first step in creating your powerful brand is to determine who you are. Remember, building your brand is about sharing your authentic self with the world. As you already know your brand is built on your skills, passions, values, and beliefs. You must know yourself if you want to build a strong personal brand.

Ask yourself:

- What unique skills do I have?
- What are my core values?
- What am I most passionate about?
- What unique experiences have shaped who I am?
- How can I most effectively serve my tribe?
- What do I have to offer that no one else does?

The answer to these questions will help shape your brand. They should help get to the core of what matters most to you and how you can add value to your tribe. Take me for example I am good at understanding technology and helping people build and accomplish their goals. My core values are my faith, family, finances, and business. I am passionate about leaving a legacy for my family, helping as many people as I can build, grow, and leave a legacy of their own.

All the ups and downs of building my businesses are not losses but a lesson in their own right. I can serve my tribe by taking everything I have learned in my journey to help people not make the same mistakes that I have. A unique perspective on how you can build your business from the ground up is different than others.

Step #2 Determine What You Want to Accomplish

Once you've identified the core of who you are, it's time to think about what you want to accomplish with your band?

Ask yourself these questions:

- What do I want to accomplish, both personally and professionally?
- What do I want to be known for?
- If I could be the go-to expert on a topic, what would it be?
- What is the main message I want to communicate?
- If I could only give one piece of advice, what would it be?

The answer to these questions will further strengthen in your mind what your brand will look like. For me, I want to accomplish helping as many people as possible build and leave a lasting legacy for the next generations.

Helping people grow their business income to replace their working income to buy back more of their time to spend with friends and family.

I want to become the go-to person for Business development. To progress in business and become successful, you must go for what you want in life and business. If you want to become successful start getting comfortable with the uncomfortable.

Step #3 Identify Your Tribe

You can't effectively serve everyone and make everyone happy. Your core tribe is your core audience. It's these people who you will serve effectively and who you will be your ideal client.

To identify your tribe ask yourself these questions:

- Who can I most effectively help?
- Who will benefit most from my skill set and knowledge?
- Who am I most passionate about serving?
- Who will be attracted most to me and my brand?

When you're figuring out your tribe, you can create an avatar. This avatar will give you an idea of your ideal client.

You will want to include the following information when creating your avatar:

- Demographics:
    - How old are they?
    - What gender are they?

- o Are they single or married or other?
- o Level of education?
- o What career are they in?
- o How much do they make?
- Hopes and dreams:
  - o What are their hopes for the future?
  - o What goals do they have?
- Challenges:
  - o What challenges are they facing?
  - o Why haven't they been able to reach their goals?

Here are a few things from my avatars. His name is Kameron he is in his 30s and is a full-time employee working on transitioning into full-time entrepreneurship. His main goal is building his brand and generating sales. He wants to have a successful business that allows him to control more of his time. Instead of building his life around work, he can build his work around his life.

He would be happy to build a community of like-minded people to grow with and generate sales with. Kameron is working on getting over his negative thinking and procrastinating when building his business. He is learning that more people are counting on him than just himself. He's been understanding who loses if he doesn't win, why he has been allowing fear to hold him back, how to stop blocking his blessings and reach for what God has in store for him.

Step #4 Find Your Unique Value Proposition

Now, you need to identify your unique service proposition (USP). Your USP is your brand summed up into a single, powerful compelling statement. That describes what you do for your tribe. This is where you want to take the answers to the previous points of your avatar and put them together. Into one brand statement that sums up who you are personally and how you serve your tribe.

A USP usually looks something like this:

"Empowering newbie entrepreneurs with business growth strategies that help build their tribe and allow them to schedule work around their life and not a life around their work." Or "I help newbie entrepreneurs with business growth strategies that help them transition from working their business part-time to becoming a full-time entrepreneur with that business." Your USP does not have to say anything about your brand.

It should get right to the heart of who you are and how you help your tribe. It could help more if you were to give your USP a name that stays in their mind. Something like "Business Growth Strategies" or scale without fail". You get the point, right? It just needs to be short and memorable to describe what you do.

Step #5 Start Treating Yourself as a Brand

Once you have identified the core of your brand and your tribe it's time to start treating yourself as the brand. So, this means every time you communicate with your tribe. Whether it be by a blog post, email, podcast, social media, post, etc. you want to stay authentic to your brand message. You want to constantly speak about the problem you solve, constantly encourage them, constantly relay the message of your brand to your tribe.

You wouldn't see Nike just suddenly switching up and talking about building a house. So, you must stay on brand when communicating with your tribe. You want to state your unique service proposition as often as possible with everything you do. I know you may not want to hear it, or you may even think others wouldn't want to hear it either. But this means you should create a strong and compelling website.

So that the website can be the central base for all your online activities, we'll talk more about this in a few. Your goal is to portray yourself as a strong brand, not just a normal person. You must treat yourself like you already are a powerful brand with a powerful message.

Step # 6 Optimize Your Website

Now, it's time to get into the fun stuff, something I love doing. Develop your online presence so that it matches your brand. You want to start with your website since this will be the central hub for everything about you and your brand. This is where people will get to know who you are and what you do. A website will also function as one of the primary ways to turn visitors into paying clients.

The first impression is everything when it comes to your website. Visitors should immediately figure out how you can help solve their problems. If they can figure that out, then most visitors won't stay on your website long.

How do you optimize a website to reflect your brand?

- Have a professional logo designed
    - This shows people you are serious about what you do and see yourself as a brand.
- Show your unique service proposition
    - It's what will draw your tribe to your website and make them want to know you and your brand a little more.
- Use professional photos
    - You can always contract a photographer but, these days most phones can take high-quality photos.
- Use testimonials
    - This shows proof that you really can solve people's problems. It's like giving your potential client the confidence to trust you.

- Give them a call to action
    - You want them to take action when they come to your site. A free resource, joining the emailing list, etc. to collect their information allowing you to stay in contact with them.
- Create a compelling about page
    - Telling your story on how you got to where you are currently today. What motivates you to serve your tribe? Why do you do what you do?
- Create a service page
    - This is for clients to hire you for your services. Which explains in detail what you offer and what is included.
- Give away free resources
    - One of the best ways to build your brand and tribe is to give away free resources on your site. This could be anything from an e-book, videos courses, checklist. Pretty much anything that can bring the visitors

some value. This also allows you to build your email list.
- Create a contact page
    - This allows visitors to contact you for any further questions or concerns.

If you check out my website www.thealexandernetworkdigital.com. Now is the time to take action and build your brand…

The truth is you have a brand whether you want it or not. Everything you post or share with your tribe either adds to or takes away from the strength of your brand. If you want to build a brand you must be intentional about the things you share and post when building your brand.

Section 2: Building an effective business plan

I'm happy to say that it's not that hard to build a brand. All you need to do is start and be intentional in the things that you share, and post and it will grow from there. Now that you have your brand for you and your business. This next section will be about building an effective business plan.

Why Do You Need a Business Plan?

A business plan will help to structure your business to support you financially. To have an impact on people around you leaving a legacy you can be proud of. Some would ask, can't you just get things up and running and adjust on the fly. Can't you learn as you go? Yes, you could do those things but, the odds that your business will fail are a lot higher. Take it from someone who came out the gate running full speed.

Not knowing where or how I was going to accomplish my goals. See, a business plan is kind of like a "crystal ball". It gives you a glimpse into the future and helps predict different outcomes. Although it's not perfect, it helps you map out where you are currently and where you are headed.

More specifically, a business plan will help you:

- Estimate the total startup cost
    - Once you know the approximate cost you can determine whether you'll need to start saving or raise funds from investors. That all depends on your beliefs and the type of business you're starting.
- Project revenues and profits
    - By defining both your market and how much of that market you expect to reach. A business plan helps you estimate your potential revenue and profits.
- Convince investors
    - If your business requires investors. A business plan shows investors that you have a clear and defined strategy for achieving success. If this strategy isn't present investors are more likely not to invest or finance your business.

- Compete from the start
    - As part of your business plan, you will be able to identify key gaps in the marketplace which your company can fill. This allows you to hit the ground running.
- Anticipate challenges
    - When you create your business plan you'll look ahead and try to identify any potential problems you might encounter, this prepares you to address these issues if they happen.

Are you starting to see the value of a business plan?

It might help to think of it in construction terms. If you were building a new house, you would use a plan of action, right? I would hope so because without a plan you would encounter all kinds of issues. Wires, pipes, walls, screws, and everything else needed to build the house could end up in the wrong place. A building plan helps keep things on track with timing and cost. The same way a business plan helps keep you on track.

It ensures that your focus is on the right things and helps you avoid the mistakes that could hurt your business. It's like the foundation of the house with a strong foundation the house will be hard to knock down. So, I'm sure by now you're wondering how do you write a business plan? What should I include? No worries we are going to cover all of that in the next few pages.

We'll go step-by-step through the process of creating a solid business plan. By the end, you'll know exactly what you need to do to create your plan.

So, let's dive in!

Before We Get Started

I know you're itching to start creating your business plan and that's great. But before getting started there are a few things you want to consider. Unfortunately, most business plans are for the most part unrealistic. It's not hard to understand why, it's exciting to start a new business. You've got big dreams, big goals, and a ton of ambition. You want to make a big impact in your market and with your tribe.

The reason behind that is, the excitement often causes new entrepreneurs to overestimate how successful they'll be and underestimate the problems they will encounter. To be effective, a business plan must be realistic. Remember, you're the one who will be pouring your time, money, and energy into the venture. Before you launch you want to be confident that you have a good chance of succeeding. So, in many ways, a business plan should help you decide whether your idea will work or not. This does not mean you need to expect or predict every risk.

There is no way you can do that if you don't have experience. However, it is important to be thoughtful, systematic, and careful as you put your plan together. You may put your business plan together and realize that the potential outcome isn't as bright as you thought. You may realize that the competition is tougher than you thought or that the market is smaller than you projected it to be and that's okay. It's a good thing to understand this at the beginning.

It forces you to go back to the drawing board and reevaluate some things. It's better to realize these things before you launch your business and spend lots of money. At a minimum, your business plan should convince you that your business will succeed. When you logically evaluate all the data you've collected in your plan, you should feel confident that you're going to achieve your goals. When you're confident you're more likely to attract people to buy into your goals and visions. So, with that being said, be patient as you create your plan.

Take the necessary time to do market research, analyze your financial needs and map out your strategy for the future. Could doing this be a pain? Yes, it could be depending on how you look at things. If you see it as something that's preventing you from getting started. Then creating a business plan will seem like it's unnecessary and worthless then it will be hard to do. But then if you view it as building a foundation for a successful, lasting, business it will change your perspective. So, I hope you see the importance of a business plan and the role it plays in your success.

Now, that we got that out the way. Let's talk about what you'll need to put into your business plan.

9 Elements of a Business Plan

There are 9 elements to an effective business plan, and we will go over all 9 in detail so let's go to work people!

Executive Summary

The first of any business will be the executive summary. You can think of it as something like a high-level snapshot of your business. This gives you a general sense of what your business is all about. What product and services do you provide, where you've been, and where you're going? This section should be around 2 pages. However, just because it's short doesn't mean it's not important.

Some investors might only want to read your executive summary at first. If the summary doesn't capture their attention, they might not read the rest of the business plan.

The small business administration recommends that your plan contain at least these six things:

1. Mission statement - a short (one paragraph) statement of your business and the goals you are pursuing.
2. General information - this information includes the founding date of the business. Names and roles of founders, how many employees you have, as well as the number of locations (if there is more the one location).
3. Company highlights – drawing attention to important growth in your business. This may include finances or any other important things your business has achieved. If possible, include the numbers as well as the charts and graphs. If you're just getting started include information from past ventures.
4. Products and services – a short description of what you sell and who your customers are. If you

haven't developed a service yet, lay out your plans for developing one.
5. Financial information – if you want funding, you'll need to layout both your financial goals as well as any sources of funding that you may already have.
6. Future plans– a quick glimpse of where you're headed with your business.

The executive summary is the introduction to the rest of your business plan. It helps readers understand your business goals and needs faster. Think of it as a detailed elevator pitch. It highlights the most important points of your business plan without going into great detail. It helps you focus on the things that will play a part in the success of your business. It's important to carefully craft your executive summary.

If it's sloppy readers may not want to read the rest. If It's not engaging or unclear, they may assume that you don't know what you are doing. The executive summary should be crisp, precise, and compelling. I would consider writing the executive summary last once you've completed the rest of the business plan. Some people may be asking why last? Well, because you'll have a better understanding of the information in the business plan. You would be able to better summarize that data for readers.

Company Overview

Next, we're going to create a quick overview of your company. This will provide them with more details showing exactly what your business does and how it is structured. Like the executive summary, this section should be relatively short. This section explains exactly what your business does.

Which includes:

- Your industry of choice
- Your primary customer base
- The challenge or pain you solve for your customers
- How you solve the challenge or pain point

Essentially, you're explaining the reason for your business's existence. You're identifying a specific customer need in a specific market and clarifying exactly how you'll meet that need. It should be clear how your business will be different from the competition in the eyes of your customer. The overview section functions as your Unique Value Proposition (UVP). It explains in detail the unique value proposition that your business offers. It will also highlight any competitive advantages you have, for example, your expertise or the physical location of your business.

In case you're struggling as I did in the beginning, try answering these questions: referring back to the building your brand section will help get things started.

- Who do you serve?
    - Working mom or dad
    - Sports enthusiast
    - New business owner
    - Try to clarify who your ideal avatar is.

- How do you serve them?
    - Do you offer a superior product?
    - Better services or products
    - Lower prices
    - A better location
    - In other words, what do you have that other companies don't?

Avoid complicated things.

Ultimately, your business exists to solve a problem. The more clarity you have on the nature of the problem and the solution you provide, the better your company overview will be.

Market Analysis

Now, let's start getting into more detail. The market analysis section of a business plan gives in-depth information about your industry, your specific market, and the competition.

If this section is done correctly, it ensures readers that you know what you're getting into. That you understand how the industry works, who the big players are, and what you need to do to not only survive but thrive in such an environment.

In your market analysis you should include the following information:

1. Key industry information
    a. What is the current size of the industry?
    b. How much it has grown in the past and what kind of future growth is projected?
    c. What kind of trends are occurring in the industry and how they affect business in that industry?

2. Target market data
   a. Data in your industry, and which customers are you targeting?
   b. What are their specific needs, and how are they currently trying to address those needs?
   c. What demographic information characterizes your target market (age, gender, income, employment, and more)?
3. Target market size?
   a. How much does your target market spend each year?
   b. How often do they purchase?
   c. When do they tend to purchase?
   d. What is the projected growth of that market?
   e. The Small Business Administration offers helpful resources regarding the specific information.
4. Market share potential
   a. What percentage of your target market do you believe you can get?

5. Barriers to entry
   a. What things might make it hard for you to enter and succeed in your target market?
   b. Will, there be a high technology cost?
   c. Are there strict regulations?
   d. Will there be any difficulty finding quality personnel?
6. Competition
   a. Who are the top competitors in your target market?
   b. What is the current market share or value?
   c. What are some of the strengths and weaknesses?
   d. In what way might this make it difficult for you to succeed?

This section will take a good amount of research, but it's time well spent. The reason I think this is because it will prepare you to succeed. The more you know about the market you're entering, and the competition you'll be facing. The more you can modify and customize your approach. This will also help investors know that you've done your research. They can be confident that you're not blindly going to start without knowing what's needed to succeed.

Organization And Management

Next, we're going to describe how your business is going to be organized and structured. The aim is to explain the role of each team member and the experience that each member brings with them. First, you want to explain the general structure of your business, both organizational terms and legal terms. Where does each stakeholder or team member fit in the overall picture of your business? Include an organizational chart that shows the roles of stakeholders or team members. Who reports to who, and other important details?

In terms of the legal setup, are you:

- LLC
- S-Corp
- C-Corp
- General partnership
- Sole proprietor

As you discuss the legal setup of your business, it should be clear who the owners are and what percentages each person owns.

Then, describe the background of key members of your team, including:

- Owners
- Board of directors
- Managers
- Partners
- Any other essential people

This part is very important if you're looking for funding. Investors want to know that you have experienced, successful individuals who can help ensure that your business succeeds. You may want to include resumes of the key members as proof of their experience.

Finally, describe key hires that will be necessary this may not be needed immediately, especially if you have everyone in place already.

Products and Services

Now, it's time to explain in detail what products or services your business will provide for customers. The goal of this section is to show how your product or service is uniquely positioned to make a splash in your target market.

Start by describing the product or service and the specific need it will meet. As much as possible try not to use industry lingo or buzzwords. Make sure your text is clear and simple for the reader to understand. It's important to clarify exactly how your product or service will stand apart from your competition. If you're selling a well-known item like phone cases or books you won't have to spend much time focusing on the details of the product itself. Instead, focus on what makes your offer unique could be the pricing or the quality of the product.

However, if you're creating something entirely new it's important to spend a good amount of time explaining exactly how your products or service works and why it's valuable. If you don't do this, readers or investors won't have enough information to make a clear evaluation of your business.

Within this section, you should include:

1. Products and services – Do you have a product or service ready to present the market, or are you still in the idea stage? It should be clear how far along your main product or service is.
2. Development objective – If your product or service isn't ready, map out the steps you will take to finish it. In detail explain the research and development actions you'll take for a product or service to be ready for the market. Also, note any future products or services you plan on developing.
3. Proprietary information – do you have any intellectual property, patents, or proprietary information that is essential to the success of your business? You want to be clear about those things in this section.
4. Supply chain – If you depend on any suppliers and vendors for any aspect of your business list the details. Include who supplies what, how often

you get supplies and the method in which you receive those supplies?

Your products and services should shine in this section. The reader should be able to understand and see that you have something unique to offer. They should also see that you're in a good position to attract customers.

Market and Sales

You've discussed the critical details about your product and services. Now, it's time to go over how you're going to get those products or services to the customers. You may have the best product or services in the world, but if you don't have a specific plan for selling it, you'll more than likely have a hard time succeeding. The objective of this section is to give readers a better understanding of how you're going to make customers aware and how they will buy from you.

Let's start by discussing marketing first.

The first step in marketing needs to be your positioning. In other words, how will you position yourself in relation to your competitors? Why should people come shop with you?

Will you position yourself by offering:

- Lower prices
- Better quality
- Better service

Next, discuss the specific promotional methods you'll use to get the word out about your product or services. Will you be using online advertisements? Do you have a content marketing plan? What systems will you use to check if your marketing efforts are working (lead generated, social media reach, website visitors, and more)?

Once you're done laying out your marketing plan, you'll want to discuss the sales plan:

1. Explain your specific sales strategy. What method will you use to convince customers to shop with you?

a. Cold calling
  b. In-person conferences
  c. Webinars or live streaming
2. Who will be doing the selling? If you need a sales team, who will train them and how does the team need to be?
3. What budget will you have for your marketing and sales? This will help readers get a better feel for your efforts and results.

Financial Projections

This is a critical section of your business plan. Here is where you paint a clear picture of your business as it is currently. While mapping out where you hope to be in the future. Investors will closely examine this section to determine if they want to give you funding. They want to be confident that your business will generate a profit, and a solid financial projection will help give them that confidence. This section will also help you get a better understanding of how successful your business can be.

If you've been in business for a little while include as much past financial data as possible like:

- Income statements
- Balance sheets
- Cashflow statements
- Operating budget
- Accounts receivable and payable statements (meaning suppliers, vendors, debtors, etc.)
- Documentation of any debt you're carrying

Your financial projections for the future will either be based on past data or industry and competitor's research.

The Small Business Administration says:

- Provide a prospective financial outlook for the next five years. Include forecasted income statements, balance sheets, cash flow statements, and capital expenditures budget (meaning the amounts and timing of certain assets purchased by the company). For the first year, be even more specific using quarterly or even monthly projections. Matching your projection to your funding request if that is the route you're going to take.

If you're not sure how to create these projections, consider hiring an accountant or a financial advisor to assist you. They will be able to further guide you in building accurate financial projections. Whenever possible you want to use graphs and charts to provide readers with a visual representation of your financial history. Also makes it easier to quickly grasp your financial situation.

Funding Request

If you're going to need funding to accomplish your business goals, be clear in what you're asking for. In this section, explain exactly how much funding you'll need over the next 5 years. Explain how you will use the funding to accomplish your goals.

Include the following details in this section:

- The amount of funding you need

- The type of funding you want (loan, investment, etc.)
- The terms you're requesting for the funding

If you're offering collateral to secure a loan, include detailed information about the collateral. Make sure it will be understood how you will use the funding. Will you need to get your items in bulk to have inventory? Paying down debt? Are you hiring some employees? If you're going to use the funding for multiple things, explain in detail how much will be used for each thing. It's critical to explain your future financial plans so investors have an idea of what they're getting into.

If you're getting a loan show how you will repay it. If your goal is to sell the business at some point, let that be known as well. As much as possible try to customize your funding request based on who you are talking to. Banks want to know that you will repay the loan, while investors want to know what kind of return, they will get on their investment. If you're asking a bank, provide them with a repayment plan. If you're asking an investor, give them an estimated return on investment (ROI).

In terms of how much funding you should request, will depend on both your needs and financial projections. You want to get enough funding to ensure that it will help your business be a success. Without asking for so much that it becomes a burden.

Appendix

You're almost done with your business plan. In this last section, you'll need to include the appendix. This final part matters just as much as the other elements of your business plan. And no, we're not talking about the appendix inside your body. We're talking about the appendix for your business plan which allows you. To include more valuable information in your business plan that doesn't interrupt the body of your business plan.

You may want to include:

- Credit history
- Permits

- Product pictures
- Legal documents
- Licenses
- Patents
- Contracts

This is also where you would include some key information and yourself and your team, such as resumes. Think of it like this, in all the other sections you're trying to paint a compelling picture of what your business is like and where it's headed. You want to give the reader enough data to help them see your vision, but not much that you push them away. At the beginning of your appendix, include a table of contents that corresponds to each section of your business plan. Allowing readers to easily see which piece of information goes with which section

Build Your Dream Business Plan

I know you're probably like man, this is a lot of work. Yes, it will take some time to create a good business plan that will convince others to support your vision. But it will be time well spent especially if you want to eventually sell the business or seek funding. Creating this business plan will give you a better understanding and a unique insight into what it will take for your business to succeed. It will push you to separate yourself from competitors. You will have a powerful marketing and sales plan in place.

You will have a better understanding of your finances in detail. If you feel like it is getting overwhelming just remember. Take it one step at a time and you will complete it in no time. You will be able to make better choices in your business like is this a good market, can I stand out and build my tribe. Or is it even worth going into that field of business? As you work on your business plan, keep your mind on the big picture. Remembering the reason, you're doing all this work is to build your dream business.

The time spend upfront on creating a business plan will be repaid in full when your business is crazy successful. Don't forget that it takes about 8 months for a house to be built from the ground up and about a month of that time is the concrete foundation being put down. So, if you want your business built on a solid foundation you want to take your time and make sure everything is down properly. So, don't wait any longer to create your business plan. Because your dream business is around the next corner! Now that have your brand and business plan in order. Let's start building a tribe of loyal supporters around your brand and business. Creating a community of like-minded people that you can grow with.

Section 3: Building Your Tribe

The Age of The Influencers

Now more than ever, we are living in the age of influencers. In past years, you had to be a well-known celebrity, politician, or a leader in your community to be considered an influencer. If you were an average person no one paid much attention to you. The path to being an influencer usually involved years of social or political ladders. But, then the internet, social media, and smartphones came along and helped change the game for influencers you don't have to be famous.

You don't have to be a good-looking person. You don't have to be well-known right away. You simply only need to know how to create engaging and meaningful content that interests people. The good thing about the internet is that it allows people to find others like them. It makes it a little easier to build a tribe around your shared interests. With every tribe, there is an influencer. There are running, finance, gaming, knitting, business, mental health, beauty, vegan, keto, fashion and so many more. You can name any subject, career, and believe there is an influencer in that arena.

This does create a challenge at times. If everyone can be an influencer, it's a little harder to stand out. It can be challenging to cut through the noise and get the attention of others. It can be hard to build an audience when others are trying to do the same thing. Building your tribe is one of the best things you can do because you will have support in everything you do. So, let's walk through the what, why, and how of becoming an influencer. You'll learn some steps and strategies for finding your tribe. Building a community or ecosystem and even how you would monetize it.

What Is an Influencer?

Before we get into the details of becoming an influencer, let's make sure we're all on the same page. At a high level, an influencer is someone who has a tribe and can influence their tribe to do different things. Like purchasing products, attending events, wearing certain items of clothing, and more. Let's call them tribers, short for members in your tribe, sounds pretty good right, just made that up. It's obvious, celebrities who have millions of tribers on social media are influencers. But you don't have to be Dwayne (The Rock) Johnson, Drake or Kanye West to be considered an influencer. Depending on your niche, you can be an influencer even if you only have 1,000 tribers.

There are 3 types of influencers:

1. Mega-influencer – these are celebrities with millions of tribers. They can charge hundreds of thousands of dollars for putting a post on their platforms. They usually will have over 1 million tribers.
2. Macro-influencer – these are individuals who are not exactly celebrities but, still have built a large community of tribers in their niche. They probably have somewhere between 50,000 to 1 million tribers. With some hard work and consistency, we can build our community of tribers the same way.

3. Micro-influencer – these are people who have built an audience in a specific niche and are known for their knowledge and expertise. Maybe they manage a sizable group or have a community of 1,000 to 50,000of tribers.

Platforms For Influencers

Most people think about influencers in terms of social media, but there are all kinds of ways you can be an influencer. If you're able to attract people you can be an influencer.

Some of the more common platforms are:

1. Blog – blogging is a great way to be an influencer because it allows you to share your expertise in a more insightful and in-depth manner.
2. YouTube – If you don't mind being engaging on camera, YouTube might be the platform for you. And in some cases, you don't even have to get on camera. There are influencers in literally every

subject you can think of, from makeup, mental health, to spreadsheets.

3. Podcasting – podcasts are exploding right now, and if you can create an interesting show that attracts listeners, brands will want to work with you.
4. Social media – social media can be both a blessing and a curse when it comes to being an influencer. There is a positive and negative to everything right?
    a. It's a blessing because there's a low barrier for entry and it's easy to create content.
    b. It's a curse because so many people use social media, and it can be a little harder to stand out.
5. Email – there has been an increase in email newsletters. If you can build a large email list and write newsletters that others want to read, this can be an effective way to become an influencer.

The point is if you can build a large community of tribers on any platform, you can become an influencer that brands want to work with. You don't need to be photogenic or able to speak the best. If you can command people's attention and move them to action, you are an influencer. Some influencers, like popular YouTubers, have a broad audience. Others speak to a smaller niche group, such as business influencers on LinkedIn.

Some focus on being fun and entertaining. Others try to deliver valuable insights and expertise. The bottom line is that no matter who you are you can be an influencer.

Benefits of Being an Influencer

There are several benefits when it comes to being an influencer. If you build up a big-enough audience, you can make a good amount of money by partnering with different brands. Even if you don't make a lot of money there are still perks:

- Build your reputation – if you consistently give your audience, your knowledge, and expertise. You'll develop a reputation as the go-to person in your industry. You may get invited to different events to speak, appear on podcasts, or do workshops with companies.
- Attract new clients – the more your reputation grows the more people will want to work with you. You'll be able to grow your business without having to constantly look for new clients.
- Connect with others – as an influencer, you can authentically connect with large numbers of people. You can build meaningful relationships that you wouldn't normally be able to do.

Becoming an influencer isn't easy and takes a good amount of work, but pays off in the long run. Whether you want to become a full-time influencer or simply boost your career, it's definitely worth the time and effort required.

Now let's get into some strategies of how to become an influencer:

9 Strategies to Building a Tribe
Step #1 Choose your niche

One of the first steps in becoming an influencer is choosing a niche. It's possible to be a "general" influencer and build a tribe. Of people who simply enjoy watching you go through life. However, this could be difficult unless you're able to make yourself stand out in some way. You'll probably have better success if you pick a specific niche in which you could build your tribe. Because you'll be making so much content in the niche, it should be something you enjoy and in which you have some expertise.

The niche you choose should be broad enough that you can build a good size community. If your niche is not scalable not enough people will be interested in the content you produce.

When choosing your niche, ask yourself these questions:

- What am I good at?
- What do I like to do?

- What problems can I help people solve?
- What value can I deliver to my tribe?
- What can I offer that no one else does?

Your goal is to find a niche that is broad enough that many people will care but, narrow enough so you can stand out. One way to do this is to start on a somewhat wide range and progressively shrink it down to a certain specialty, or subcategory of the broader niche. For example, say you're a therapist some sub-topics fall under the category of therapy. Including marriage, work, parenting, relationships, health, weight loss, and many more.

Instead of trying to cover all these subjects, pick one to focus on in the beginning. As you start to grow your tribe, you can start to expand into other sub-topics. It will be helpful to do some research before choosing the niche you want to operate in. A simple way to do research is to search different platforms for answers to common. Challenges that your tribe struggles with. For example, if you're a career coach you could search YouTube for tips on finding new jobs.

If you're a financial advisor, you could search Facebook or Instagram for financial advice. A google search can also help find the most popular websites in your niche. The search results will help you learn who the influencers in that niche are and the kind of content they produce. Armed with this information you can determine whether a particular niche is for you. For me, my niche is helping new entrepreneurs transition from working their business part-time to working it full-time. Allowing them to schedule their work around their life instead of scheduling their life around their work.

Step #2 Define Your Tribe

Once you've determined your niche, it's important to define your tribe. In other words, you want to be clear on who is in your niche and what they care about. Knowing your tribe allows you to create content that is valuable to them. If you are not clear on your tribe, you may end up creating irrelevant content. Which can make it harder for you to attract your tribe.

To help you define your tribe, think through these questions:

- What is their age range?
- What are their hopes and dreams?
- What do they fear?
- What motivates them?
- What do they want out of life?
- What are their biggest struggles?
- What or who do they look up to?
- What do they dislike?
- Whose opinion influences them?
- Where do they go for information?

If you're not sure about the answers to any of these questions, you can post them on social media. To see what kind of feedback you get from the post. This can give you insight into how your audience thinks.

Facebook Audience Insight can also be helpful when it comes to understanding your tribe. It provides a collection of data about the preferences of a specific group of people. You can see the pages they like, education level, relationship status, and much more. Another way to get more insight into the mind of a triber is to join relevant online groups. Paying attention to what members discuss most in the group.

What topics are talked about most? What common problems do people in the group struggle with? What specific words and phrases do they use? You may be tempted to skip this step, thinking you already know your tribe. But this will help you get a better understanding of what's good and what's not when deciding on what content you want to post. With the right content, you will be able to build a tribe much faster.

Step #3 Pick a Platform

Once you define your niche and start building your tribe, you're in a good place to choose a platform. You may think you should be present in as many places as possible, but this isn't usually a good idea. You'll end up getting spread too thin, and your overall impact will be watered down. Choose at least one or two platforms where you will focus most of your attention. The platforms you choose should be in alignment with the type of content you produce.

For example:

- If you're a writer, you may want to create a website where you can blog regularly.
- If you're brand is more visual, Instagram will work great for you.
- If you're a video creator, you should focus on YouTube.

- If you're in more of a business-to-business (B2B) industry, LinkedIn will work great for you.

Take me for example I'm active on LinkedIn, YouTube, and Instagram. If you're not sure which platform works best for you keep your tribe in mind. Where do they spend more of their time? What apps are being used more often? Who are they following on social media? What platform do they follow them on? You want to be where your tribe is.

Also, what platform do other influencers use in your niche? Being on the same platform allows you to interact with those influencers. Which could open more doors and opportunities for collaboration. In addition to choosing a primary platform, will benefit you to choose a supporting platform where you'll share smaller pieces of content. For example, you're a blogger you may want to utilize Facebook or LinkedIn. Where you can share snippets of your blog post and link them back to your website.

If you're a video creator like me, you may want to use Instagram or Facebook. To share short clips from your longer-form video post and link them back to YouTube for the full video. As much as possible you want to use your supporting platform to drive people back to the primary platform. For example, if you share short clips of a video from YouTube to Instagram, add a link to the full video on the comment's notes, or a caption to encourage people to watch the full video on YouTube.

As you grow your tribe you can expand to other platforms for more exposure. In the beginning, it makes more sense to focus on a couple of platforms.

Step #4 Spice UP Your Social Media Profiles

You'll want to make the best out of your social media platforms. To make them stand out from the crowd. When people visit your accounts, give them a great first impression so that they'll want to follow you.

Try these easy strategies to make your accounts stand out:

1. Add a good profile picture – Your profile picture is an important part of your brand and identity. Use a high-quality picture that matches your personality. Avoid low-quality pictures that may be blurry or have bad lighting.
2. Add a cover photo – a solid cover photo allows you to give more information about yourself. Things like your motto, places you've been featured, media outlets, or even a picture of you with

friends or family. Pretty much it should help explain your overall brand.
3. Switch to a business account – almost every social media platform has a business account option. When you do this, you get access to more features, such as analytics and advertising.
4. Craft a compelling bio – your bio communicates who you are and what your mission is. It should be done in a manner that is authentically you and attracts and interest people. Include relevant keywords, so you appear in searches.
5. Untag yourself from negative posts – most platforms allow others to tag you in posts. If you're tagged in negative posts, like inappropriate photos, be sure to untag yourself.
6. Pin your best content – most social media platforms allow you to pin your best content to the top of your profile. Pin the

post that best shows who you are and the value you offer.

Depending on the platform you choose, there is another way to spice up your profile. For example, YouTube allows you to add an introductory video to your channel. Which is a great way to let others get to know you. LinkedIn lets you add in some resume information. Take advantage of all these additional features. I'm working on building up my YouTube, Facebook, and Instagram now.

Step #5 Map Out Your Content

Before you start creating and posting content, it's best to develop an overall content strategy. Mapping out your content will help to know what to post and when to post it. It will also help if you find yourself creatively blocked at any point. As you think through your content, consider your tribe. Your goal is to provide content that is valuable to your tribe and allows you to show your personality. Both of those are very important when building your tribe.

If you're not providing valuable content, people will have no reason to be a part of your tribe. If you don't show your personality, you won't stand out from other influencers who are sharing similar content. The combination of value and personality is what will help you rise to the top.

Creating High-Value Content

What makes a piece of content valuable? That depends on what your tribe wants.

Content is valuable to your tribe if it:

- Helps them solve a problem
- Gives them valuable knowledge
- Brings out emotions
- Entertains them
- Makes their life better in some way

All sorts of content can meet these requirements. Everything from video tutorials, nice pictures, or a meme can be valuable to your tribe. It just needs to add value to them in some way. Luckily, we don't have to create all of this ourselves. The best influencers also share valuable content created by others. This also can get you noticed by whoever created the content, which can open some relational doors.

One effective strategy for content is the 5-3-2 principle. For every 10 social media posts:

- 5 are by someone else
- 3 are valuable content you created
- 2 are about you

Using this strategy ensures that you don't get overwhelmed with content creation. It establishes your know, like, and trust factor and helps your tribe get to know you better.

Finding Content Ideas

If you're having trouble with coming up with ideas. There are a few strategies you can use, such as:

- Type relevant phrases into Google and look at the related searches at the bottom of the page. This will give you a sense of the different things your tribe is searching for that are related to the main topic you typed in.
- Answer the public is another helpful tool for content ideas. You type in a set of keywords, and it spits out a list. Of commonly asked questions related to the keyword.
- Quora can be helpful with coming up with ideas. If you type in keywords, it will show you related questions, people have posted on the website. If you select one of the questions, you can see all the answers provided.

Step #6 Publish Your Content

After mapping out your content strategy, you're finally ready to start publishing. If you want your content to be seen, it's important to post consistently. When it comes to social media, most platforms prefer active accounts. For a deeper look at the best times to post on each social media platform, read this article. Generally, the best day to post is Wednesday and the most engagement happens between the late morning and middle of the afternoon.

That being said, don't get held up on posting at the perfect time. You'll have the most success just posting constantly throughout the week.

Using Social Media Scheduler

If you're like most of us, the thought of having to log in and post multiple times per week would probably be overwhelming. After all, you've got a lot going on. This is where social media scheduling tools can be very helpful. They allow you to schedule your posts in advance and then automatically publish them for you.

Some of the best social media schedulers are:

- Content Studios
- Buffer
- Hootsuite
- Coschedule
- Sprout Social

With these tools, you can create a posting schedule, fill your queue with posts, and have the platform publish them when the time comes.

Optimizing Your Posts

Optimizing each of your posts for the platform it is being published. A video clip on Instagram looks different than a video clip on Facebook. Photos on Facebook look different than photos on Twitter. Make sure that each post looks great on the platform it's published on.

Your post should also be optimized for mobile devices as well. With the majority of people consuming content on mobile devices, you'll want to make sure that your posts look good on mobile, desktop, and tablets. Another way to optimize your post is to use hashtags. Hashtags allow other people to find posts related to specific subjects that a person may be interested in. For example, if someone wants to find an Instagram post about small businesses. They will search using the hashtag #smallbusiness. So doing hashtag research is a great way to reach more people.

Using relevant hashtags on your posts can help you get discovered by people who wouldn't otherwise know about you.

If you're not sure which hashtags to use, these tools can help:

- All hashtags
- Ritetag
- Instavast Hashtag Generator
- #hashtag

Step #7 Engage with Your Audience

The importance of engaging with your audience can be underestimated. The engagement just means interacting with your tribe, in ways like. Responding to their comments, answering their questions, and more. Influencers who engage get more traction faster than those who don't interact. If you're not willing to engage with your tribe regularly. You'll most likely struggle to succeed in becoming an influencer.

Why is engagement so important you might ask? Great question.

Consider these reasons:

1. Engagement allows you to build a positive relationship with people in your tribe. When you reply to comments, answer questions, and provide helpful resources, it helps your tribe to trust you more. They can see that you're a genuine person who cares about them.
    a. If you don't engage with your tribe, you'll seem more like a corporate person than an authentic person. People want to feel like they know you and will be less interested in following you or your brand.
2. Almost every social media platform boost post that has a lot of engagement. When they see a post with lots of comments and likes it's a signal to them that the content is valuable, and more people should see it. The more engagement you have on a post, the more people will see it.

3. Comments on your post give you more insight into the different ways your tribe thinks. You can see and hear what they want in their own words. You'll have a better understanding of what drives them and learn how you can better serve them.

Yes, it can take some time to reply to comments and have meaningful conversations, but it's worth it. Your tribe will see you as more authentic and you'll get a nice boost from social media algorithms.

Step #8 Analyze Your Results

One of the biggest keys to succeeding as an influencer is regularly analyzing your results. You want to know what kind of content impacts your tribe most and gets the most interaction. So, if you want to work with brands, it's important to be able to give them concrete data about the content you produce. They will want to know the size of your tribe and how much engagement your post gets. If you can't give them that information, most brands won't feel confident that they'll get much return on investment (ROI) from working with you.

Every platform offers analytics of some kind that you can use to evaluate your post.

You'll want to compile this type of data:

- If you're a blogger, you'll want to analyze how many people visit your site, which pages they visit most, how long they stay on those sites, and more.
- If you're a podcaster, take a close look at the number of downloads you're getting per episode and which episodes get the most downloads.
- If you're using YouTube look into your overall subscriber growth, which videos get the most views, how long people watch your videos, and similar statistics.

- On social media, analyze which posts get the most likes, comments, and repost. Also, look at the demographics of your tribe.

As you check your results, pay close attention to content that performs well, as well as the comments left by your tribe. This information shows you what matters most to your tribe. If a blog post, video, podcast episode, or social media post performs well, think about doubling down on that type of content. As you focus on more of the content that performs best, you'll pick up momentum, and your tribe will grow faster.

Step #9 Collaborate with Brands

The Final Step in being an influencer is working with brand in exchange for products or money. How do I connect with these brands you might ask?

There are several ways you can connect:

1. You can wait for brands to reach out to you. If your tribe is big enough, you will eventually be noticed by brands who are interested in working with you. Make sure that you put your contact information on all your online profiles. So, it's easier for brands to get in touch with you.
2. Consistently tagging brands and products you want to work with in your post is a way to get the attention of companies showing them that you are open to collaborating. It's not the quickest approach but can have good results over the long run.
3. If you want to take a more proactive approach, think about reaching out to relevant companies that align with your brand message. When you do this be clear about the value you can bring to them. You'll want to give statistics about the

size of your tribe and the type of engagement your content gets.
   a. To Save time think about creating a template that you can use multiple times.
4. Use an influencer platform, these platforms serve as a marketplace, bringing together influencers and companies interested in working with you. There are tons of different influencer platforms out there including:
   a. Activate
   b. AspireIQ
   c. Find Your Influencer
   d. Grin
   e. Hypr
   f. And many more

You'll need to spend some time researching which platform is right for you. Some are more focused and cater to a certain audience, while others are much broader. Find the strategy that works for you and start working with brands.

The Conclusion

In closing, we broke the book down into three sections, and what I learned and am still learning about that brought value to my business. In the first section, we discussed how everyone has a personal brand whether they created it or not. So, being intentional about building your brand is very important if you want to go far. In the summary we talked about different strategies on how to:

- Identify what matters to you
- Defining your core tribe
- Determining your unique service proposition (USP)
- Treating yourself like a brand
- Creating a compelling website
- Being your authentic self consistently

The more you work on doing these things, the more you'll build your brand and attract your tribe. In the second section, we discuss different strategies on how to build an effective business plan. We know that creating a business plan can be a lot of work, but in the long run, it can help take you to the next level. Allowing you to see ways to separate yourself from your competitors. So, don't feel overwhelmed just remember to take it one day at a time and be authentic and truthful in the process. Stay focused on getting one step done at a time:

1. Step #1 Executive Summary (Which you will have to do last when creating but is the first thing that needs to be seen)
2. Company Overview
3. Market Analyses
4. Organization and Management
5. Production and Services
6. Marketing and Sales
7. Financial Projections
8. Funding Request
9. Appendix

Do one step, then the next, then the next, and before you know it the entire business plan will be completed. While you're working on your business plan remember to keep the big picture in mind. The reason you're doing the work is so you can build your dream business. The time spent upfront creating your business plan will be repaid in full, and some, when your business is successful. In the last section, we discussed strategies on how to build a tribe around your brand and the business of loyal supporters. We discussed a few different strategies like:

- What is an influencer and the benefits of being an influencer?
- Choosing your niche
- Defining your tribe
- Picking your primary platform
- Spicing up your social media profiles
- Mapping out your content
- Publishing your content
- Engaging with your audience
- Analyzing your results

- Collaborating with brands

Becoming an influencer doesn't happen overnight. You must be consistent in your content and build the know, like, and trust factor in your tribe. So that you are the go-to person for your niche.

So, let's not wait any longer to build your business. You have the strategies to take your business to the next level so let's get to it and build that dream business. I also want to thank you for taking the time out to read this book. As I build my brand and business, I wanted to share with my tribe the things I have been learning that have helped me and I feel that it could help so many others. Thank you again and hope to see you at the top remember, you can't rush the process you have to trust the process. Go through each phase and help someone else along the way that is the only way we can grow together.

Additional Resources

My name is Kameron Alexander I was born and raised in Rockford, Illinois. I was a smart and quiet kid growing up I was known as the cool kid with glasses. Never really played any sports but liked math and computers in school. I like to travel and spend time with friends and family. I have some college experience in IT engineering and diplomacy in business administration. I'm currently building a digital marketing agency that helps newbie entrepreneurs with business development, digital marketing, and wealth-building strategies.

I like to call myself a business coach because that is what I want to do. And this book is one of the first steps in that direction. I want to help tons of newbie entrepreneurs that are working their full-time job with a side business. Transition into working the side business full-time and buying back their time. Instead of scheduling their life around their work, they can schedule their work around their life.

I've been married since July 2015 and I absolutely love being married to my beautiful wife Anais love you, babe. To my kids who have been the highlight of my life. Helping me become the man I am today, knowing that I must set a good example for them so that they know what a good husband, father, son, friend, and just an all-around good person looks like. I love you kids more than you will ever know.

Resources

- Alexander Network Digital - https://www.thealexandernetworkdigital.com/
- Small Business Administration - https://www.sba.gov/business-guide/plan-your-business/market-research-competitive-analysis
- Facebook Audience Insight - https://www.facebook.com/business/insights/tools/audience-insights
- Answer the public - https://answerthepublic.com/
- Quora - https://www.quora.com/
- Post times - https://sproutsocial.com/insights/best-times-to-post-on-social-media/
- Content Studios - https://contentstudio.io/?fpr=alexandernetwork
- Buffer - https://buffer.com/
- Hootsuite - https://www.hootsuite.com/
- Coscheduler - https://coschedule.com/
- Sprout Social - https://sproutsocial.com/

- Allhashtags - https://www.all-hashtag.com/
- Ritetag - https://ritetag.com/
- Instavast Hashtag Generator - https://instavast.com/instagram-hashtag-generator/
- #Hashtag - https://hashmeapp.com/index.html
- Active - https://try.activate.social/
- AspireIQ - https://aspire.io/
- Find Your Influencer - https://findyourinfluence.com/
- Grin - https://grin.co/
- Hypr - https://www.juliusworks.com/

**Some links are affiliate links in which a may earn a small commission. **

www.ingramcontent.com/pod-product-compliance
Lightning Source LLC
Chambersburg PA
CBHW070132100426
42744CB00009B/1811